Introduction

Whether you enjoy making dishcloths for a local charity, to give as a hostess or shower gift or just to enjoy using yourself, this book is for you!

Rather than using and reusing the same pattern to make your dishcloths, spice up your crochet time with our creative stitch patterns and new design ideas. Use the colors shown, or use any color that sparks your interest. The decision is yours. As you try each pattern, you will be building on your crochet skills while you make a block that is fresh and fun.

The real bonus is how these great cotton cloths make dishwashing time more enjoyable. And when they get dirty, you can put them in the washer and dryer so they are as good as new.

So, pick up some inexpensive worsted weight cotton yarn and a crochet hook, and you'll always have a great "take-along" project to make your day fly by!

Design Directory

Dippity Doos

Page 4

Serenity

Page 10

Precision

Page 6

This Way & That

Page 12

Sand & Sea

Page 8

Tri-Color Hexagon

Page 14

Pretty Posy

Page 16

Rib Hexagon

Page 22

Sunshine

Page 18

Nestling Shells

Page 24

Harmony

Page 20

Sassy Shells

Page 27

Skill Level
◧■□▯ EASY

Finished Size
Approximately 11½ x 11½ inches

Materials
- Medium (worsted) weight cotton yarn (2½ oz/ 120 yds/70g per ball): 1 ball each blue *(A)* and yellow *(B)*
4 MEDIUM
- Sizes G/6/4mm and H/8/5mm crochet hooks or size needed to obtain gauge
- Tapestry needle

Gauge
Size H hook: 6 sts = 2 inches

Special Stitch
Long double crochet (long dc): Yo, draw up lp to height of working row in sp indicated, [yo, draw through 2 lps on hook] twice.

Pattern Note
To change color, work last stitch until 2 loops remain on hook; with new color, yarn over and draw through 2 loops on hook. Drop old color.

Instructions

Center
Row 1 (RS): With H hook and A, ch 33; dc in 4th ch from hook *(beg 3 sk chs count as a dc)* and in next ch; [ch 1, sk next ch, dc in next 3 chs] 7 times, turn. *(7 ch-1 sps)*

Row 2: Ch 3 *(counts as a dc on this and following rows)*, dc in next 2 dc; [ch 1, dc in next 3 dc] 6 times; ch 1, dc in next 2 dc and in 3rd ch of beg 3 sk chs, changing to B in last dc; drop A, turn.

Row 3: Ch 4 *(counts as a dc and a ch-1 sp on this and following rows)*, sk next dc; *dc in next dc, working over next ch-1 sp, **long dc** *(see Special Stitch)* in ch-1 sp on 2nd row below, dc in next dc, ch 1, sk next dc; rep from * 6 times; dc in 3rd ch of turning ch-3, turn.

Row 4: Ch 4, sk next ch-1 sp, dc in next 3 dc; *ch 1, sk next ch-1 sp, dc in next 3 dc; rep from * 6 times; ch 1, sk next ch-1 sp, dc in 3rd ch of turning ch-4, changing to A; drop B, turn.

Row 5: Ch 3; *working over next ch-1 sp, long dc in ch-1 sp on 2nd row below, dc in next dc, ch 1, sk next dc, dc in next dc; rep from * 6 times; working over next ch-1 sp, long dc in ch-1 sp on 2nd row below, dc in 3rd ch of turning ch-4, turn.

Row 6: Ch 3, dc in next 2 dc; [ch 1, dc in next 3 dc] 6 times; ch 1, dc in next 2 dc and in 3rd ch of turning ch-3, changing to B in last dc; drop A, turn.

Rows 7–18: [Work rows 3–6] 3 times. Fasten off and weave in ends.

Edging
Rnd 1 (RS): Hold piece with RS facing you and row 18 at top; with G hook and A make slip knot on hook and join with sc in first dc in upper right-hand corner; 2 sc in same dc—*beg corner made*; work 29 sc evenly spaced to last st, 3 sc in last st—*corner made*; *working across next side in ends of rows, work 29 sc evenly spaced to beg ch; working across next side in unused lps of beg ch, 3 sc in first lp—*corner made*; work 29 sc evenly spaced to last lp; 3 sc in last lp—*corner made*; working across next side in ends of row, work 29 sc evenly spaced to joining sc; join with sl st in joining sc. *(128 sc)*

Rnd 2: Ch 5, sl st in 3rd ch from hook—*beg picot made*; [hdc in next sc, ch 3, sl st in 3rd ch from hook—*picot made*] twice; *sk next sc; [hdc in next sc, picot, sk next sc] 14 times; in each of next 3 sc work (hdc, picot); rep from * twice; sk next sc; [hdc in next sc, picot, sk next sc] 14 times; join in 2nd ch of beg ch-5.
Fasten off and weave in ends. ●

Skill Level
 ◼◼☐☐ EASY

Finished Size
Approximately 11 x 11 inches

Materials
- Medium (worsted) weight cotton yarn (2½ oz/ 120 yds/70g per ball): 1 ball each blue *(A)*, white *(B)* and green *(C)*
- Sizes G/6/4mm and H/8/5mm crochet hooks or size needed to obtain gauge
- Tapestry needle

Gauge
Size H hook: 6 sts = 2 inches

Special Stitch
Front post double crochet (fpdc): Yo, insert hook from front to back around **post** *(see Stitch Guide)* of st indicated; draw lp through, [yo, draw through 2 lps on hook] twice.

Instructions

Center
Row 1 (RS): With H hook and C, ch 34; sc in 2nd ch from hook and in each rem ch across, turn. *(33 sc)*

Row 2: Ch 3 *(counts as a dc on this and following rows)*, dc in each rem sc, turn.

Row 3: Ch 1, sc in each dc and in 3rd ch of turning ch-3. Fasten off.

Row 4: Hold piece with RS facing you; with H hook and A make slip knot on hook and join with sc in first sc; sc in next 2 sc; *[**fpdc** *(see Special Stitch)* around post of next dc on 2nd row below] 3 times; on working row, sc in next 3 sc; rep from * 4 times, turn.

Row 5: Ch 3, dc in each st, turn.

Row 6: Ch 1, sc in each dc and in 3rd ch of turning ch-3. Fasten off.

Row 7: Hold piece with RS facing you; with H hook and B make slip knot on hook and join with sc in first sc; sc in next 2 sc; *fpdc around post of each of next 3 dc on 2nd row below, on working row, sc in next 3 sc; rep from * 4 times, turn.

Row 8: Ch 3, dc in each st, turn.

Row 9: Ch 1, sc in each dc and in 3rd ch of turning ch-3. Fasten off.

Rows 10–12: With C, rep rows 7–9.

Rows 13–21: Rep rows 4–12.

Rows 22–28: Rep rows 4–10. Fasten off and weave in ends.

Edging
Rnd 1 (RS): Hold piece with RS facing you and row 28 at top; with G hook and B, make slip knot on hook and join with sc in first sc in upper right-hand corner; 2 sc in same sc—*beg corner made*; sc in next 31 sts, 3 sc in next sc—*corner made*; working across next side in ends of rows, work 30 sc evenly spaced to beg ch; working across next side in unused lps of beg ch, 3 sc in first lp—*corner made*; sc in each lp to last lp; 3 sc in last lp—*corner made*; work across next side in ends of rows, work 30 sc evenly spaced to joining sc; change to A by drawing lp through; cut B; join with sl st in joining sc. *(134 sc)* Turn.

Rnd 2: Ch 1, sc in first sc, tr in next sc; *sc in next sc, tr in next sc; rep from * around; join with sl st in first sc.

Fasten off and weave in ends. ●

Sand & Sea

Skill Level

 EASY

Finished Size
Approximately 11½ x 11½ inches

Materials
- Medium (worsted) weight cotton yarn (2½ oz/ 120 yds/70g per ball): 1 ball each taupe (A) and blue (B)
- Sizes G/6/4mm and H/8/5mm crochet hooks or size needed to obtain gauge
- Tapestry needle

Gauge
Size H hook: 6 sts = 2 inches

Special Stitches
V-Stitch (V-st): In st indicated work (dc, ch 1, dc).
Beginning shell (beg shell): Ch 3, 4 dc in st indicated.
Shell: 5 dc in st indicated.

Pattern Note
To change color, work last stitch until 2 loops remain on hook; with new color, yarn over and draw through 2 loops on hook. Cut old color.

Instructions

Center
Row 1 (RS): With H hook and A, ch 32; sc in 2nd ch from hook; *ch 1, sk next 2 chs, in next ch work **V-st** (see Special Stitches); ch 1, sk next 2 chs, sc in next ch; rep from * 4 times, changing to B in last sc; cut A, turn. (5 V-sts)
Row 2: Ch 3 (counts as a dc on this and following rows), dc in first sc, [ch 1, sc in ch-1 sp of next V-st, ch 1, V-st in next sc] 4 times; ch 1, sc in ch-1 sp of next V-st, ch 1, 2 dc in last sc, changing to A; cut B, turn.
Row 3: Ch 1, sc in first dc, [ch 1, V-st in next sc, ch 1, sc in ch-1 sp of next V st] 4 times; ch 1, V-st in next sc, ch 1, sc in 3rd ch of turning ch-3, changing to B; cut A, turn.
Rows 4–19: [Work rows 2 and 3] 8 times.
Fasten off and weave in ends.

Edging
Rnd 1 (RS): Hold piece with RS facing you and row 19 at top; with G hook and A make slip knot on hook and join with sc in first sc in upper right-hand corner; 2 sc in same sc—beg corner made; work 28 sc evenly spaced across to last sc; 3 sc in last sc—corner made; working across next side in ends of rows, work 28 sc evenly spaced to beg ch; working across next side in unused lps of beg ch, 3 sc in first lp—corner made; work 28 sc evenly spaced to last lp; 3 sc in last lp—corner made; working across next side in ends of rows, work 28 sc evenly spaced to joining sc, changing to B in last sc; cut A; join with sl st in joining sc. (124 sc)
Rnd 2: Sl st in next sc; **beg shell** (see Special Stitches) in same sc; *sk next sc, sc in next sc, sk next sc, **shell** (see Special Stitches) in next sc, sk next sc, sc in next sc, sk next 2 sc, [shell in next sc, sk next 2 sc, sc in next sc, sk next 2 sc] 3 times; shell in next sc; sk next sc, sc in next sc, sk next sc, shell in next sc; rep from * twice; sk next sc, sc in next sc, sk next sc, shell in next sc; sk next sc, sc in next sc, sk next 2 sc, [shell in next sc, sk next 2 sc, sc in next sc, sk next 2 sc] 3 times; shell in next sc; sk next sc, sc in next sc, sk next sc; join with sl st in 3rd ch of beg ch-3. Fasten off.
Rnd 3: With G hook, join A in any sc; ch 3 (counts as a dc), 3 dc in same sc; *sk next 2 dc of next shell, sc in next dc, 4 dc in next sc; rep from * to last shell; sk next 2 dc of last shell, sc in next dc; join with sl st in 3rd ch of beg ch-3.
Fasten off and weave in ends. ●

Skill Level

◼◼◻◻ EASY

Finished Size

Approximately 11½ x 11½ inches

Materials

- Medium (worsted) weight cotton yarn (2½ oz/ 120 yds/70g per ball): 1 ball cream *(A)* and teal *(B)*

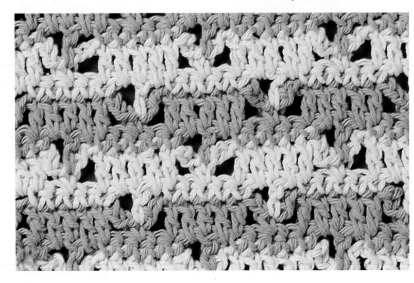

4 MEDIUM

- Sizes G/6/4mm and H/8/5mm crochet hooks or size needed to obtain gauge
- Tapestry needle

Gauge

Size H hook: 6 sts = 2 inches

Pattern Note

To change color, work last stitch until 2 loops remain on hook; with new color, yarn over and draw through 2 loops on hook. Cut or carry old color.

Instructions

Center

Row 1 (RS): With H hook and B, ch 34; sc in 2nd ch from hook; *ch 3, sk next ch, dc in next 5 chs, ch 3, sk next ch, sc in next ch; rep from * across, changing to A in last sc; cut B, turn.

Row 2: Ch 4 *(counts as a dc and a ch-1 sp on this and following rows)*; *sc in next 5 dc, ch 1, dc in next sc, ch 1; rep from * twice; sc in next 5 dc, ch 1, dc in last sc, turn.

Row 3: Ch 3 *(counts as a dc on this and following rows)*, dc in next ch-1 sp and in next dc; *ch 3, sk next sc, sc in next sc, ch 3, sk next sc, dc in next dc, in next ch-1 sp, in next dc, in next ch-1 sp and in next sc; rep from * twice; ch 3, sk next sc, sc in next sc, ch 3, sk next sc, dc in next dc, in next ch-1 sp and in 3rd ch of turning ch-4, changing to B in last dc; carry A, turn.

Row 4: Ch 1, sc in first 3 dc; *ch 1, dc in next sc, ch 1, sc in next 5 dc; rep from * twice; ch 1, dc in next sc, ch 1, sc in last dc and in 3rd ch of turning ch-3, turn.

Row 5: Ch 3, sk next sc, dc in next sc, in next ch-1 sp, in next dc, in next ch-1 sp and in next sc; *ch 3, sk next sc, sc in next sc, ch 3, sk next sc, dc in next sc, in next ch-1 sp, in next dc, in next ch-1 sp and in next dc; rep from * twice; ch 3, sc in last sc, changing to A; cut B, turn.

Rows 6–21: [Work rows 2–5] 4 times. At end of row 21, do not change color.

Fasten off and weave in ends.

Edging

Rnd 1 (RS): Hold piece with RS facing you and row 21 at top; with G hook and A, make slip knot on hook and join with sc in 3rd ch of turning ch-3 in upper right-hand corner; 2 sc in same ch—*beg corner made*; work 30 sc evenly spaced to last sc; 3 sc in last sc—*corner made*; working across next side in ends of rows, work 30 sc evenly spaced to beg ch; working in unused lps of beg ch, 3 sc in first lp—*corner made*; work 30 sc evenly spaced to last lp; 3 sc in last lp—*corner made*; working across next side in ends of rows, work 30 sc evenly spaced to joining sc; join with sl st in joining sc.

Rnd 2: Ch 1, sc in same sc, ch 4; *sc in next sc, ch 4; rep from * around; join with sl st in first sc. Fasten off and weave in ends. ●

This Way & That

Skill Level
 ■■□□ EASY

Finished Size
Approximately 11½ x 11½ inches

Materials
- Medium (worsted) weight cotton yarn (2½ oz/ 120 yds/70g per ball):
    1 ball each white *(A)* and red *(B)*
- Sizes G/6/4mm and H/8/5mm crochet hooks or size needed to obtain gauge
- Tapestry needle

Gauge
Size H hook: 6 sts = 2 inches

Special Stitch
V-Stitch (V-st): In st indicated work (dc, ch 3, dc).

Pattern Note
To change color, work last stitch until 2 loops remain on hook; with new color, yarn over and draw through 2 loops on hook. Carry old color.

Instructions

Center
Row 1: With H hook and A, ch 37; in 2nd ch from hook work (sc, ch 3, 3 dc); sk next 4 chs; *in next ch work (sc, ch 3, 3 dc); sk next 4 chs; rep from * to last ch; sc in last ch, turn.

Row 2: Ch 3 *(counts as a dc on this and following rows)*, 3 dc in first sc; *in next ch-3 sp work (sc, ch 3, 3 dc); rep from * 5 times; sc in next ch-3 sp, ch 2, tr in last sc, **changing** to B; carry A, turn.

Row 3: Ch 1, sc in first tr; *in next sc work **V-st** *(see Special Stitch)*; sc in next ch-3 sp; rep from * 5 times; in next sc work V-st; sc in 3rd ch of turning ch-3, turn.

Row 4: Ch 5; *sc in ch-3 sp of next V-st, ch 5; rep from * 5 times; sc in ch-3 sp of next V-st, ch 2, tr in last sc, changing to A; carry B, turn.

Row 5: Ch 1, sc in first tr, 3 dc in next ch-2 sp; *sc in 3rd ch of next ch-5 sp, ch 3, 3 dc in same ch-5 sp; rep from * 5 times; sc in sp formed by turning ch-5, turn.

Rows 6–17: [Work rows 2–5] 3 times.

Row 18: Rep row 2.

Row 19: Ch 1, sc in first tr, ch 4; *sc in next ch-3, ch 4; rep from * 5 times; sc in 3rd ch of turning ch-3.

Fasten off and weave in ends.

Edging
Rnd 1: Hold piece with RS facing you and row 19 at top; with G hook and A make slip knot on hook and join with sc in first sc in upper right-hand corner; 2 sc in same sc—*beg corner made;* work 34 sc evenly spaced to last sc; 3 sc in last sc—*corner made;* working across next side in ends of row, work 34 sc evenly spaced to beg ch; working in unused lps of beg ch, 3 sc in first lp—*corner made;* work 34 sc evenly spaced to last lp; 3 sc in last lp—*corner made;* working across next side in ends of rows, work 34 sc evenly spaced to joining sc; join with sl st in joining sc. *(148 sc)*

Rnd 2: Ch 1, sc in same sc; ch 3, sl st in 3rd ch from hook—*picot made;* sk next sc; *sc in next sc, picot, sk next sc; rep from * around; join with sl st in first sc.

Fasten off and weave in ends. ●

Tri-Color Hexagon

Skill Level
 ◼◼◻◻ EASY

Finished Size
Approximately 13 inches from
point to point

Materials
- Medium (worsted) weight
  cotton yarn (2½ oz/
  120 yds/70g per ball):
  1 ball each white (A),
  cream (B) and taupe (C)
- Size H/8/5mm crochet hook or
  size needed to obtain gauge
- Tapestry needle

4 MEDIUM

Gauge
6 sts = 2 inches

Special Stitches
Beg popcorn (beg pc): Ch 3, 4 dc
in sp indicated, remove hook and
insert it in 3rd ch of beg ch-3 and
in top lp of 4th dc made, yo and
draw through both lps on hook.

Popcorn (pc): 5 dc in sp indicated,
remove hook and insert it in
top lp of first and 5th dc made,
yo and draw through both lps
on hook.

Instructions

Center
Rnd 1: With H hook and A, ch 2; 12
sc in 2nd ch from hook; join with
sl st in first sc. Fasten off.

Rnd 2: With H hook, join B in any
sc; ch 5 (counts as a dc and a ch-2
sp), [dc in next sc, ch 2] 11 times;
join with sl st in 3rd ch of beg
ch-5. Fasten off.

Rnd 3: With H hook, join C in
any ch-2 sp; **beg pc** (see Special
Stitches) in same sp; ch 3; *pc (see
Special Stitches) in next ch-2 sp;
ch 3; rep from * 10 times; join with
sl st in beg pc. (12 pcs) Fasten off.

Rnd 4: With H hook, join A with
sl st in any ch-3 sp; ch 3, 3 dc in
same sp; ch 1, [4 dc in next ch-3
sp, ch 1] 11 times; join in 3rd ch of
beg ch-3. Fasten off.

Rnd 5: With H hook, join B with
sl st in any ch-1 sp; ch 3, 3 dc in
same sp; *in next ch-1 sp work
(4 dc, ch 2, 4 dc)—corner made;
4 dc in next ch-1 sp; rep from * 4
times; in next ch-1 sp work (4 dc,
ch 2, 4 dc)—corner made; join in
3rd ch of beg ch-3. Fasten off.

Rnd 6: With H hook, join C with
sl st in sp after last 4-dc group of
any corner and next 4-dc group;

ch 3, 3 dc in same sp; *4 dc in sp
between same dc group and
4-dc group of next corner; in ch-2
sp of corner work corner; 4 dc in
sp between next 4-dc group of
corner and next 4-dc group; rep
from * 4 times; 4 dc in sp between
same dc group and 4-dc group of
next corner; in ch-2 sp of corner
work corner; join with sl st in 3rd
ch of beg ch-3. Fasten off.

Rnd 7: With H hook, join A with sl
st in sp after last 4 dc group of
any corner and next 4-dc group,
ch 3, 3 dc in same sp; [4 dc in next
sp between same 4-dc group and
next 4-dc group] twice; *corner
in next corner; [4 dc in next sp
between same 4-dc group and
next 4-dc group] 3 times; rep
from * 4 times; corner in next
corner; join with sl st in 3rd ch of
beg ch-3. Fasten off.

Rnd 8: With H hook, join B with sl
st in sp after last 4 dc group of
any corner and next 4-dc group,
ch 3, 3 dc in same sp; [4 dc in
next sp between same 4-dc
group and next 4-dc group] 3
times; *corner in next corner; [4
dc in next sp between same 4-dc
group and next 4-dc group] 4
times; rep from * 4 times; corner
in next corner; join with sl st in
3rd ch of beg ch-3. Fasten off.

Rnd 9: With H hook and C, make
slip knot on hook and join with
sc in same ch as joining of rnd 8;
*sc in each dc to ch-2 sp of next
corner; 2 sc in ch-2 sp; rep from
* 5 times; sc in each dc to first sc;
join with sl st in first sc.
Fasten off and weave in ends. ●

Pretty Posy

Finished Size

Approximately 13 inches from picot to picot

Materials

- Medium (worsted) weight cotton yarn (2½ oz/ 120 yds/70g per ball): 1 ball each hot pink *(A)*, pink *(B)* and white *(C)*
- Size H/8/5mm crochet hook or size needed to obtain gauge
- Tapestry needle

Gauge

6 sts = 2 inches

Instructions

Center

Rnd 1 (RS): With A, ch 5; join with sl st to form ring; ch 3 *(counts as a dc on this and following rnds)*, 15 dc in ring; join with sl st in 3rd ch of beg ch-3. *(16 dc)*

Rnd 2: Ch 1, sc in same ch as joining; ch 5, sk next dc; *sc in next dc, ch 5, sk next dc; rep from * around; join with sl st in first sc. Fasten off.

Rnd 3: Join B with sl st in any ch-5 sp; ch 3, in same sp work (7 dc, ch 5, sl st in top of last dc made—*picot made*; 7 dc)—*petal made*; in each rem ch-5 sp work (7 dc, picot, 7 dc)—*petal made*; join with sl st in 3rd ch of beg ch-3. *(8 petals)* Fasten off.

Rnd 4: Working behind petals, with C make slip knot on hook and join with sc in any sc on rnd 3; ch 5; *sc in next sc between petals, ch 5; rep from * around; join with sl st in first sc.

Rnd 5: Sl st in next ch-5 sp; ch 3, 5 dc in same sp; 6 dc in each rem ch-5 sp; join with sl st in 3rd ch of beg ch-3.

Rnd 6: Sl st in next dc; ch 3, in same dc work (dc, ch 1, 2 dc); sk next 2 dc, in next dc work (2 dc, ch 1, 2 dc); sk next 2 dc; rep from * around; join with sl st in 3rd ch of beg ch-3.

Rnd 7: Sl st in next dc and in next ch-1 sp; ch 3, in same sp work (2 dc, ch 1, 3 dc); in each rem ch-1 sp work (3 dc, ch 1, 3 dc); join with sl st in 3rd ch of beg ch-3.

Rnd 8: Sl st in next 2 dc and in next ch-1 sp; ch 3, in same sp work (3 dc, ch 2, 4 dc); in each rem ch-1 sp work (4 dc, ch 2, 4 dc); join with sl st in 3rd ch of beg ch-3. Fasten off.

Rnd 9: Join B with sl st in any ch-2 sp; ch 3, in same sp work (4 dc, picot, 5 dc); in each rem ch-2 sp work (5 dc, picot, 5 dc); join with sl st in 3rd ch of beg ch-3.

Fasten off and weave in ends. ●

Sunshine

Skill Level
 EASY

Finished Size
Approximately 10½ x 10½ inches

Materials
- Medium (worsted) weight cotton yarn (2½ oz/ 120 yds/70g per ball): 1 ball orange (A)
- Medium (worsted) weight cotton yarn (1½ oz/68 yds/42g per ball): 1 ball yellow/white/orange variegated (B)
- Sizes G/6/4mm and H/8/5mm crochet hooks or size needed to obtain gauge
- Tapestry needle

Gauge
Size H hook: 6 sts = 2 inches

Special Stitch
Front post double crochet (fpdc): Yo, insert hook from front to back to front around **post** (see Stitch Guide) of st indicated, draw lp through, [yo, draw through 2 lps on hook] twice.

Instructions

Center
Rnd 1: With H hook and B, ch 5; join with sl st to form ring; ch 6 (counts as a dc and a ch-3 sp), 2 dc in ring; ch 3, [3 dc in ring, ch 3] 3 times; join with sl st in 3rd ch of beg ch-6. Fasten off.

Rnd 2: With H hook, join A with sl st in any ch-3 sp; ch 3 (counts a dc on this and following rnds), 2 dc in same sp; [**fpdc** (see Special Stitch) around post of each of next 3 dc; in next ch-3 sp work (3 dc, ch 3, 3 dc)—corner made] 3 times; fpdc around post of each of next 3 dc; 3 dc in same ch-3 sp as beg ch-3 made; ch 3; join with sl st in 3rd ch of beg ch-3. Fasten off.

Rnd 3: With H hook, join B with sl st in any corner ch-3 sp; ch 3 (counts as a dc on this and following rnds), 2 dc in same ch-3 sp; *dc in next 3 dc, fpdc around each of next 3 fpdc, dc in next 3 dc, in next corner ch-3 sp work corner; rep from * twice; dc in next 3 dc, fpdc around each of next 3 fpdc, dc in next 3 dc, 3 dc in same sp as beg ch-3 made; ch 3; join with sl st in 3rd ch of beg ch-3. Fasten off.

Rnd 4: With H hook, join A with sl st in any corner ch-3 sp; ch 3, 2 dc in same ch-3 sp; *dc in next 6 dc, fpdc around each of next 3 fpdc, dc in next 6 dc, corner in next corner; rep from * twice; dc in next 6 dc, fpdc around each of next 3 fpdc; dc in next 6 dc, 3 dc in same ch-3 sp as beg ch-3 made; ch 3; join with sl st in 3rd ch of beg ch-3. Fasten off.

Rnd 5: With H hook, join B with sl st in any corner ch-3 sp; ch 3, 2 dc in same sp; *dc in next 9 dc, fpdc around each of next 3 fpdc, dc in next 9 dc, corner in next corner; rep from * twice; dc in next 9 dc, fpdc around each of next 3 fpdc; dc in next 9 dc, 3 dc in same sp as beg ch-3 made; ch 3; join with sl st in 3rd ch of beg ch-3. Fasten off.

Rnd 6: With H hook, join A with sl st in any corner ch-3 sp; ch 3, 2 dc in same sp; *dc in next 12 dc, fpdc around each of next 3 fpdc, dc in next 12 dc, corner in next corner; dc in next 12 dc, fpdc around each of next 3 fpdc, dc in next 12 dc, 3 dc in same sp as beg ch-3 made; ch 3; join with sl st in 3rd ch of beg ch-3. Fasten off.

Rnd 7: With H hook, join B with sl st in any corner ch-3 sp; ch 3, 2 dc in same ch-3 sp; *dc in next 15 dc, fpdc around each of next 3 fpdc, dc in next 15 dc, corner in next corner; rep from * twice; dc in next 15 dc, fpdc around each of next 3 fpdc, dc in next 15 dc, 3 dc in same sp as beg ch-3 made; ch 3; join with sl st in 3rd ch of beg ch-3.

Rnd 8: With G hook and A, make slip knot on hook and join with sc in corner ch-3 sp; 2 sc in same sp; *sc in each st to next corner ch-3 sp; 3 sc in corner ch-3 sp; rep from * twice; sc in each st to joining sc; join with sl st in joining sc.

Fasten off and weave in ends. ●

Harmony

Skill Level
■■□□ **EASY**

Finished Size
Approximately 10½ x 10½ inches

Materials
• Medium (worsted) weight yarn (2½ oz/120 yds/70g per ball):
  1 ball pink
• Sizes G/6/4mm and H/8/5mm crochet hooks or size needed to obtain gauge
• Tapestry needle

Gauge
Size H hook: 6 sts = 2 inches

Special Stitches
Cluster (cl): Keeping last lp of each dc on hook, dc in 3 sts indicated, yo and draw through all 4 lps on hook.

Front post double crochet (fpdc): Yo, insert hook from front to back to front around **post** (see Stitch Guide) of st indicated, draw lp through, [yo, draw through 2 lps on hook] twice.

Instructions

Center
Row 1 (RS): With H hook, ch 37; **cl** (see Special Stitches) in 6th, 7th and 8th chs from hook; *ch 1, dc in next ch, ch 1, cl in next 3 chs; rep from * 6 times; dc in last ch, turn.

Row 2: Ch 1, sc in first dc, ch 1; *sc in next cl, ch 1, sc in next dc; rep from * 6 times; sc in next cl, ch 1, sk next ch of beg 5 sk chs, sc in next ch, turn.

Row 3: Ch 4 (counts as a dc and a ch-1 sp on this and following rows); *cl in next ch-1 sp, next sc and next ch-1 sp; ch 1, **fpdc** (see Special Stitches) around post of next dc on 2nd row below; ch 1; rep from * 6 times; cl in next ch-1 sp, next sc and next ch-1 sp; ch 1, sc in last sc, turn.

Row 4: Ch 1, sc in first dc, ch 1; *sc in next cl, ch 1, sc in next dc; rep from * 6 times; sc in next cl, ch 1, sc in 4th ch of turning ch-4, turn.

Row 5: Ch 4; *cl in next ch-1 sp, next sc and next ch-1 sp; ch 1, fpdc around next fpdc on 2nd row below; ch 1; rep from * 6 times; cl in next ch-1 sp, next sc and next ch-1 sp; ch 1, sc in last sc, turn.

Rows 6–21: [Work rows 2 and 3] 8 times.
Fasten off and weave in ends.

Edging
Rnd 1: Hold piece with RS facing you and row 21 at top; with G hook make slip knot on hook and join with sc in first st in upper right-hand corner; 2 sc in same st—beg corner made; work 31 sc evenly spaced to last st; 3 sc in last st—corner made; working across next side in ends of rows, work 31 sc evenly spaced to beg ch; working in unused lps of beg ch, 3 sc in first lp—corner made; work 31 sc evenly spaced to last lp; 3 sc in last lp—corner made; working across next side in ends of rows, work 31 sc evenly spaced to joining sc; join with sl st in joining sc.

Rnd 2: Ch 1, sc in same sc as joining; ch 3, sk next sc; *sc in next sc, ch 3, sk next sc; rep from * around; join with sl st in first sc.
Fasten off and weave in ends. ●

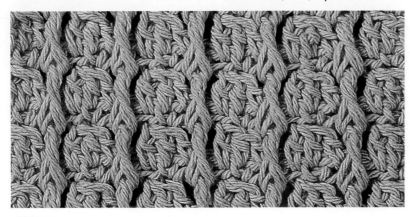

Rib Hexagon

Skill Level

■■□□ EASY

Finished Size

Approximately 12 inches from point to point

Materials

- Medium (worsted) weight cotton yarn (2 oz/ 95 yds/56g per ball): 1 ball blue/green/yellow variegated

- Size H/8/5mm crochet hook or size needed to obtain gauge
- Tapestry needle

Gauge

6 sts = 2 inches

Special Stitches

Back post double crochet (bpdc): Yo, insert hook from back to front to back around **post** (see Stitch Guide) of st indicated, draw lp through, [yo, draw through 2 lps on hook] twice.

V-stitch (V-st): In sp indicated work (dc, ch 1, dc).

Instructions

Center

Rnd 1 (RS): Ch 4; 11 dc in 4th ch from hook (beg 3 sk chs count as a dc); join with sl st in 3rd ch of beg ch-4, turn. (12 dc)

Rnd 2: Sl st in next ch-1 sp; ch 4 (counts as a dc and a ch-1 sp on this and following rnds), dc in same sp; *bpdc (see Special Stitches) around post of each of next 2 dc; in sp between last dc and next dc work V-st (see Special Stitches); rep from * 4 times; bpdc around post of each of next 2 dc; join with sl st in 3rd ch of beg ch-4.

Rnd 3: Sl st in next ch-1 sp, ch 4, dc in same sp; *bpdc around each of next 4 dc, V-st in ch-1 sp of next V-st; rep from * 4 times; bpdc around each of next 4 dc; join with sl st in 3rd ch of beg ch-4.

Rnd 4: Sl st in next ch-1 sp, ch 4, dc in same sp; *bpdc around each of next 6 dc, V-st in ch-1 sp of next V-st; rep from * 4 times; bpdc around each of next 6 dc; join with sl st in 3rd ch of beg ch-4.

Rnd 5: Sl st in next ch-1 sp, ch 4, dc in same sp; *bpdc around each of next 8 dc, V-st in ch-1 sp of next V-st; rep from * 4 times; bpdc around each of next 8 dc; join with sl st in 3rd ch of beg ch-4.

Rnd 6: Sl st in next ch-1 sp, ch 4, dc in same sp; *bpdc around each of next 10 dc, V-st in ch-1 sp of next V-st; rep from * 4 times; bpdc around each of next 10 dc; join with sl st in 3rd ch of beg ch-4.

Rnd 7: Sl st in next ch-1 sp, ch 4, dc in same sp; *bpdc around each of next 12 dc, V-st in ch-1 sp of next V-st; rep from * 4 times; bpdc around each of next 12 dc; join with sl st in 3rd ch of beg ch-4.

Rnd 8: Sl st in next ch-1 sp, ch 4, dc in same sp; *bpdc around each of next 14 dc, V-st in ch-1 sp of next V-st; rep from * 4 times; bpdc around each of next 14 dc; join with sl st in 3rd ch of beg ch-4.

Rnd 9: Sl st in next ch-1 sp, ch 4, dc in same sp; *bpdc around each of next 16 dc, V-st in ch-1 sp of next V-st; rep from * 4 times; bpdc around each of next 16 dc; join with sl st in 3rd ch of beg ch-4.

Rnd 10: Sl st in next ch-1 sp, ch 4, dc in same sp; *bpdc around each of next 18 dc, V-st in ch-1 sp of next V-st; rep from * 4 times; bpdc around each of next 18 dc; join with sl st in 3rd ch of beg ch-4.

Rnd 11: Sl st in next ch-1 sp, ch 4, dc in same sp; *bpdc around each of next 20 dc, V-st in ch-1 sp of next V-st; rep from * 4 times; bpdc around each of next 20 dc; join with sl st in 3rd ch of beg ch-4.

Fasten off and weave in ends. ●

Nestling Shells

Skill Level

 EASY

Finished Size

Approximately 10½ x 10½ inches

Materials

- Medium (worsted) weight cotton yarn (2½ oz/ 120 yds/70g per ball): 1 ball green
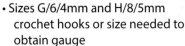
- Sizes G/6/4mm and H/8/5mm crochet hooks or size needed to obtain gauge
- Tapestry needle

Gauge

Size H hook: 6 sts = 2 inches

Special Stitches

Shell: In st indicated work (3 dc, ch 1, 3 dc).

Back post double crochet (bpdc): Yo, insert hook from back to front to back around **post** (see Stitch Guide) of st indicated, draw lp through, [yo, draw through 2 lps on hook] twice.

Front post double crochet (fpdc): Yo, insert hook from front to back to front around **post** (see Stitch Guide) of st indicated, draw lp through, [yo, draw through 2 lps on hook] twice.

V-stitch (V-st): In st indicated work (dc, ch 1, dc).

Instructions

Center

Row 1: With H hook, ch 39; dc in 4th ch from hook (beg 3 sk chs count as a dc); *sk next 3 chs, in next ch work **shell** (see Special Stitches); sk next 3 chs, dc in next 2 chs; rep from * across, turn. (4 shells)

Row 2: Ch 4 (counts as a dc and a ch-1 sp on this and following rows), dc in first dc; ch 1, **bpdc** (see Special Stitches) around post of next dc; *sc in ch-1 sp of next shell, sk next 3 dc of same shell, bpdc around post of next dc, ch 1, in sp between same 2 dc work **V-st** (see Special Stitches); ch 1, bpdc around post of next dc; rep from * twice; sc in ch-1 sp of next shell, sk next 3 dc of same shell, bpdc around post of next dc, ch 1, in 3rd ch of beg 3 sk chs work (dc, ch 1, dc), turn.

Row 3: Ch 4, 2 dc in next ch-1 sp; *fpdc (see Special Stitches) around each of next 2 bpdc; in ch-1 sp of next V-st work (2 dc, ch 3, 2 dc); rep from * twice; fpdc around each of next 2 bpdc, 2 dc in sp formed by turning ch-4; dc in 3rd ch of same turning ch-4, turn.

Row 4: Ch 4, 3 dc in next ch-1 sp; *bpdc around each of next 2 fpdc, shell in next ch-3 sp; rep from * twice; bpdc around each of next 2 fpdc, ch 1, dc in 3rd ch of turning ch-4, turn.

Row 5: Ch 1, sc in first dc, fpdc around next bpdc; *ch 1, V-st in sp between same bpdc and next bpdc, ch 1, fpdc around next bpdc, sc in ch-1 sp of next shell; rep from * twice; ch 1, V-st in sp between same bpdc and next bpdc, ch 1, fpdc around next bpdc, sc in 3rd ch of turning ch-4, turn.

Row 6: Ch 3 (counts as a dc on this and following rows), bpdc around next fpdc; *in ch-1 sp of next V-st work (2 dc, ch 3, 2 dc); bpdc around each of next 2 fpdc; rep from * twice; in ch-1 sp of next V-st work (2 dc, ch 3, 2 dc); bpdc around last fpdc, dc in last sc, turn.

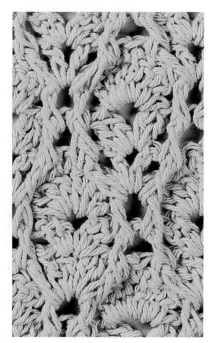

Row 7: Ch 3, fpdc around next bpdc; *shell in next ch-2 sp; fpdc around each of next 2 bpdc; rep from * twice; shell in next ch-2 sp; fpdc around next bpdc, dc in 3rd ch of turning ch-3, turn.

Row 8: Ch 4, dc in first dc; ch 1, bpdc around next fpdc; *sc in ch-1 sp of next shell, sk next 3 dc of same shell, bpdc around post of next fpdc, ch 1, V-st in sp between same 2 dc; ch 1, bpdc around post of next fpdc; rep from * twice; sc in ch-1 sp of next shell, sk next 3 dc of same shell, bpdc around post of next fpdc, ch 1, in 3rd ch of turning ch-3 work (dc, ch 1, dc), turn.

Rows 9–14: Rep rows 3–8.

Rows 15 & 16: Rep 3 and 4. Fasten off and weave in ends.

Edging

Rnd 1: Hold piece with RS facing you and row 16 at top; with G hook make slip knot on hook and join with sc in first st in upper right-hand corner; 2 sc in same st—*beg corner made*; work 32 sc evenly spaced to last st; 3 sc in last st—*corner made*; working across next side in ends of rows, work 32 sc evenly spaced to beg ch; working across next side in unused lps of beg ch, 3 sc in first lp—*corner made*; work 32 sc evenly spaced to last lp; 3 sc in last lp—*corner made*; working across next side in ends of rows, work 32 sc evenly spaced to joining sc; join with sl st in joining sc.

Rnd 2: Ch 2 (*counts as a hdc*), 3 hdc in next sc—*corner made*; hdc in each sc to 2nd sc of next corner; 3 hdc in 2nd sc—*corner made*; rep from * twice; hdc in each sc to beg ch-2; join with sl st in 2nd ch of beg ch-2.

Rnd 3: Ch 1, working left to right, work **reverse sc** (*see below*) in each hdc; join with sl st in first reverse sc.

Fasten off and weave in ends. ●

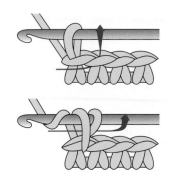

Reverse Single Crochet

Sassy Shells

Skill Level
 ■■□□ EASY

Finished Size
Approximately 11½ x 11½ inches

Materials
- Medium (worsted) weight cotton yarn (2½ oz/ 120 yds/70g per ball): 1 ball each white *(A)*, green *(B)* and hot pink *(C)*
- Sizes G/6/4mm and H/8/5mm crochet hooks or size needed to obtain gauge
- Tapestry needle

Gauge
Size H hook: 6 sts = 2 inches

Special Stitches
Shell: In st indicated work 5 dc.
Long double crochet (long dc): Yo, draw up lp to height of working row in st or sp indicated, [yo, draw through 2 lps on hook] twice.
Beginning V-stitch (beg V-st): Ch 3, hdc in same st indicated.
V-stitch (V-st): In st indicated work (hdc, ch 1, hdc).

Pattern Note
To change color, work last stitch until 2 loops remain on hook; with new color, yarn over and draw through 2 loops on hook. Cut old color.

Instructions

Center
Row 1 (RS): With H hook and C, ch 34; 2 dc in 4th ch from hook *(beg 3 sk chs count as a dc)*; *ch 1, sk next 5 chs, in next ch work **shell** (see Special Stitches); rep from * 4 times; ch 1, sk next 2 chs, 3 dc in last ch, **changing** to B in last dc; cut C, turn.

Row 2: Ch 1, sc in first dc, ch 1; *working over next ch-1 sp, **long dc** (see Special Stitches) in 4th sk ch of next 5 sk chs on beg ch, ch 1, working over same ch-1 sp and in front of last long dc made, long dc in 2nd sk ch of same 5 sk chs on beg ch, ch 1, sk next 2 dc of next shell, sc in next dc, ch 1; rep from * 3 times; working over next ch-1 sp, long dc in 4th sk ch of next 5 sk chs on beg ch, ch 1, working over same ch-1 sp and in front of last long dc made, long dc in 2nd sk ch of same 5 sk chs on beg ch, ch 1, sk next 2 dc, sc in 3rd ch of beg 3 sk chs, turn.

Row 3: Ch 1, sc in first sc; *shell in ch-1 sp between next 2 long dc; ch 1; rep from * 3 times; shell in ch-1 sp between next 2 long dc; sc in last sc, changing to A; cut B, turn.

Row 4: Ch 3 *(counts as a dc on this and following rows)*, dc in first sc; *ch 1, sk next 2 dc of next shell, sc in next dc, ch 1, working over next ch-1 sp, long dc in ch-1 sp to left of next sc on 2nd row below, ch 1, working over same ch-1 sp and in front of last long dc made, long dc in ch-1 sp to right of same sc on 2nd row below; rep from * 3 times; ch 1, sk next 2 dc of next shell, sc in next dc, ch 1, 2 dc in last sc, turn.

Row 5: Ch 3, 2 dc between first and 2nd dc; *ch 1, shell in ch-1 sp between next 2 long dc; rep from * 3 times; ch 1, 3 dc between last 2 dc, changing to C in last dc; cut A, turn.

Row 6: Ch 1, sc in first dc; *ch 1, working over next ch-1 sp, long dc in ch-1 sp to left of next sc on 2nd row below, ch 1, working over same ch-1 sp and in front of last long dc made, long dc in ch-1 sp to right of same sc on 2nd row below; rep from * 4 times; ch 1, sk next 2 dc, sc in 3rd ch of turning ch-3, turn.

Row 7: Ch 1, sc in first sc; *shell in ch-1 sp between next 2 long dc; ch 1; rep from * 3 times; shell in ch-1 sp between next 2 long dc; sc in last sc, changing to B; cut C, turn.

Row 8: Ch 3, dc in first sc; *ch 1, sk next 2 dc of next shell, sc in next dc, ch 1, working over next ch-1 sp, long dc in ch-1 sp to left of next sc on 2nd row below, ch 1, working over same ch-1 sp and in front of last long dc made, long dc in ch-1 sp to right of same sc on 2nd row below; rep from * 3 times; ch 1, sk next 2 dc of next shell, sc in next dc, ch 1, 2 dc in last sc, turn.

Row 9: Ch 3, 2 dc between first and 2nd dc; *ch 1, shell in ch-1 sp between next 2 long dc; rep from * 3 times; ch 1, 3 dc between last 2 dc, changing to A in last dc; cut B, turn.

Row 10: Ch 1, sc in first dc; *ch 1, working over next ch-1 sp, long dc in ch-1 sp to left of next sc on 2nd row below, ch 1, working over same ch-1 sp and in front of last long dc made, long dc in ch-1 sp to right of same sc on 2nd row below; rep from * 4 times; ch 1, sk next 2 dc, sc in 3rd ch of turning ch-3, turn.

Row 11: Ch 1, sc in first sc; *shell in ch-1 sp between next 2 long dc; ch 1; rep from * 3 times; shell in ch-1 sp between next 2 long dc; sc in last sc, changing to C; cut A, turn.

Row 12: Ch 3, dc in first sc; *ch 1, sk next 2 dc of next shell, sc in next dc, ch 1, working over next ch-1 sp, long dc in ch-1 sp to left of next sc on 2nd row below, ch 1, working over same ch-1 sp and in front of last long dc made, long dc in ch-1 sp to right of same sc on 2nd row below; rep from * 3 times; ch 1, sk next 2 dc of next shell, sc in next dc, ch 1, 2 dc in last sc, turn.

Row 13: Ch 3, 2 dc between first and 2nd dc; *ch 1, shell in ch-1 sp between next 2 long dc; rep from * 3 times; ch 1, 3 dc between last 2 dc, changing to B in last dc; cut C, turn.

Row 14: Ch 1, sc in first dc; *ch 1, working over next ch-1 sp, long dc in ch-1 sp to left of next sc on 2nd row below, ch 1, working over same ch-1 sp and in front of last long dc made, long dc in ch-1 sp to right of same sc on 2nd row below; rep from * 4 times; ch 1, sk next 2 dc, sc in 3rd ch of turning ch-3, turn.

Row 15: Ch 1, sc in first sc; *shell in ch-1 sp between next 2 long dc; ch 1; rep from * 3 times; shell in ch-1 sp between next 2 long dc; sc in last sc, changing to A; cut B, turn.

Row 16: Ch 3, dc in first sc; *ch 1, sk next 2 dc of next shell, sc in next dc, ch 1, working over next ch-1 sp, long dc in ch-1 sp to left of next sc on 2nd row below, ch 1, working over same ch-1 sp and in front of last long dc made, long dc in ch-1 sp to right of same sc on 2nd row below; rep from * 3 times; ch 1, sk next 2 dc of next shell, sc in next dc, ch 1, 2 dc in last sc, turn.

Row 17: Ch 3, 2 dc between first and 2nd dc; *ch 1, shell in ch-1 sp between next 2 long dc; rep from * 3 times; ch 1, 3 dc between last 2 dc, changing to C in last dc; cut A, turn.

Row 18: Ch 1, sc in first dc; *ch 1, working over next ch-1 sp, long dc in ch-1 sp to left of next sc on 2nd row below, ch 1, working over same ch-1 sp and in front of last long dc made, long dc in ch-1 sp to right of same sc on 2nd row below; rep from * 4 times; ch 1, sk next 2 dc, sc in 3rd ch of turning ch-3, turn.

Row 19: Ch 1, sc in first sc; *shell in ch-1 sp between next 2 long dc; ch 1; rep from * 3 times; shell in ch-1 sp between next 2 long dc; sc in last sc.

Fasten off and weave in ends.

Edging

Rnd 1 (RS): Hold piece with RS facing you and row 19 at top; with G hook and A make slip knot on hook and join with sc in first sc in upper right-hand corner; 2 sc in same sc—*beg corner made*; *work 29 sc evenly spaced to last sc; 3 sc in last st—*corner made*; working across next side in ends of rows, work 29 sc evenly spaced to beg ch; working in unused lps of beg ch, 3 sc in first lp—*corner made*; work 29 sc evenly spaced to last lp; 3 sc in last lp—*corner made*; working across next side in ends of rows, work 29 sc evenly spaced to first sc; join with sl st in first sc. *(128 sc)*

Rnd 2: Beg V-st *(see Special Stitches)* in same sc; sk next sc; *in next sc work **V-st** *(see Special Stitches)*; sk next sc; rep from * around; join with sl st in 2nd ch of beg ch-3. *(64 V-sts)*

Rnd 3: Sl st in next ch-1 sp, 5 sc in same ch-1 sp; sc in ch-1 sp of next V st; *5 sc in ch-1 sp of next V st; sc in ch-1 sp of next V-st; rep from * around; join with sl st in first sc.

Fasten off and weave in ends. ●

General Information

Standard Yarn Weight System
Categories of yarn, gauge ranges, and recommended hook sizes

Yarn Weight Symbol & Category Names	1 SUPER FINE	2 FINE	3 LIGHT	4 MEDIUM	5 BULKY	6 SUPER BULKY
Type of Yarns in Category	Sock, Fingering, Baby	Sport, Baby	DK, Light Worsted	Worsted, Afghan, Aran	Chunky, Craft, Rug	Bulky, Roving
Crochet Gauge* Ranges in Single Crochet to 4 inch	21–32 sts	16–20 sts	12–17 sts	11–14 sts	8–11 sts	5–9 sts
Recommended Hook in Metric Size Range	2.25–3.25mm	3.5–4.5mm	4.5–5.5mm	5.5–6.5mm	6.5–9mm	9mm and larger
Recommended Hook U.S. Size Range	B/1–E/4	E/4–7	7–I/9	I/9–K/10½	K/10½–M/13	M/13 and larger

* **GUIDELINES ONLY:** The above reflect the most commonly used gauges and hook sizes for specific yarn categories.

Skill Levels

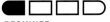

BEGINNER

Beginner projects for first-time crocheters using basic stitches. Minimal shaping.

EASY

Easy projects using basic stitches, repetitive stitch patterns, simple color changes and simple shaping and finishing.

INTERMEDIATE

Intermediate projects with a variety of stitches, mid-level shaping and finishing.

EXPERIENCED

Experienced projects using advanced techniques and stitches, detailed shaping and refined finishing.

How to Check Gauge

A correct stitch-gauge is very important. Please take the time to work a stitch-gauge swatch about 4 x 4 inches. Measure the swatch. If the number of stitches and rows is fewer than indicated under "Gauge" in the pattern, your hook is too large. Try another swatch with a smaller size hook. If the number of stitches and rows is more than indicated under "Gauge" in the pattern, your hook is too small. Try another swatch with a larger size hook.

Symbols

* An asterisk (or double asterisk **) is used to mark the beginning of a portion of instructions to be worked more than once; thus, "rep from * twice more" means after working the instructions once, repeat the instructions following the asterisk twice more (3 times in all).

[] Brackets are used to enclose instructions that should be worked the exact number of times specified immediately following the brackets, such as "[2 sc in next dc, sc in next dc] twice."

[] Brackets and () parentheses are used to provide additional information to clarify instructions.

STITCH GUIDE

Need help? ▶ **StitchGuide.com** • ILLUSTRATED GUIDES • HOW-TO VIDEOS

STITCH ABBREVIATIONS

beg	begin/begins/beginning
bpdc	back post double crochet
bpsc	back post single crochet
bptr	back post treble crochet
CC	contrasting color
ch(s)	chain(s)
ch-	refers to chain or space previously made (i.e., ch-1 space)
ch sp(s)	chain space(s)
cl(s)	cluster(s)
cm	centimeter(s)
dc	double crochet (singular/plural)
dc dec	double crochet 2 or more stitches together, as indicated
dec	decrease/decreases/decreasing
dtr	double treble crochet
ext	extended
fpdc	front post double crochet
fpsc	front post single crochet
fptr	front post treble crochet
g	gram(s)
hdc	half double crochet
hdc dec	half double crochet 2 or more stitches together, as indicated
inc	increase/increases/increasing
lp(s)	loop(s)
MC	main color
mm	millimeter(s)
oz	ounce(s)
pc	popcorn(s)
rem	remain/remains/remaining
rep(s)	repeat(s)
rnd(s)	round(s)
RS	right side
sc	single crochet (singular/plural)
sc dec	single crochet 2 or more stitches together, as indicated
sk	skip/skipped/skipping
sl st(s)	slip stitch(es)
sp(s)	space(s)/spaced
st(s)	stitch(es)
tog	together
tr	treble crochet
trtr	triple treble
WS	wrong side
yd(s)	yard(s)
yo	yarn over

YARN CONVERSION

OUNCES TO GRAMS	GRAMS TO OUNCES
1 .... 28.4	25 .... ⅞
2 .... 56.7	40 .... 1⅔
3 .... 85.0	50 .... 1¾
4 .... 113.4	100 .... 3½

UNITED STATES		UNITED KINGDOM
sl st (slip stitch)	=	sc (single crochet)
sc (single crochet)	=	dc (double crochet)
hdc (half double crochet)	=	htr (half treble crochet)
dc (double crochet)	=	tr (treble crochet)
tr (treble crochet)	=	dtr (double treble crochet)
dtr (double treble crochet)	=	ttr (triple treble crochet)
skip	=	miss

Single crochet decrease (sc dec): (Insert hook, yo, draw lp through) in each of the sts indicated, yo, draw through all lps on hook.

Example of 2-sc dec

Half double crochet decrease (hdc dec): (Yo, insert hook, yo, draw lp through) in each of the sts indicated, yo, draw through all lps on hook.

Example of 2-hdc dec

Reverse single crochet (reverse sc): Ch 1, sk first st, working from left to right, insert hook in next st from front to back, draw up lp on hook, yo and draw through both lps on hook.

Chain (ch): Yo, pull through lp on hook.

Single crochet (sc): Insert hook in st, yo, pull through st, yo, pull through both lps on hook.

Double crochet (dc): Yo, insert hook in st, yo, pull through st, [yo, pull through 2 lps] twice.

Double crochet decrease (dc dec): (Yo, insert hook, yo, draw lp through, yo, draw through 2 lps on hook) in each of the sts indicated, yo, draw through all lps on hook.

Example of 2-dc dec

Front loop (front lp) Back loop (back lp)

Front Loop   Back Loop

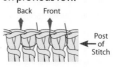

Front post stitch (fp): Back post stitch (bp): When working post st, insert hook from right to left around post of st on previous row.

Back   Front

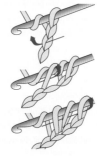

Post of Stitch

Half double crochet (hdc): Yo, insert hook in st, yo, pull through st, yo, pull through all 3 lps on hook.

Double treble crochet (dtr): Yo 3 times, insert hook in st, yo, pull through st, [yo, pull through 2 lps] 4 times.

Treble crochet decrease (tr dec): Holding back last lp of each st, tr in each of the sts indicated, yo, pull through all lps on hook.

Example of 2-tr dec

Slip stitch (sl st): Insert hook in st, pull through both lps on hook.

Chain color change (ch color change) Yo with new color, draw through last lp on hook.

Double crochet color change (dc color change) Drop first color, yo with new color, draw through last 2 lps of st.

Treble crochet (tr): Yo twice, insert hook in st, yo, pull through st, [yo, pull through 2 lps] 3 times.

Inches Into Millimeters & Centimeters

All measurements are rounded off slightly.

inches	mm	cm	inches	cm	inches	cm	inches	cm
⅛	3	0.3	5	12.5	21	53.5	38	96.5
¼	6	0.6	5½	14	22	56.0	39	99.0
⅜	10	1.0	6	15.0	23	58.5	40	101.5
½	13	1.3	7	18.0	24	61.0	41	104.0
⅝	15	1.5	8	20.5	25	63.5	42	106.5
¾	20	2.0	9	23.0	26	66.0	43	109.0
⅞	22	2.2	10	25.5	27	68.5	44	112.0
1	25	2.5	11	28.0	28	71.0	45	114.5
1¼	32	3.8	12	30.5	29	73.5	46	117.0
1½	38	3.8	13	33.0	30	76.0	47	119.5
1¾	45	4.5	14	35.5	31	79.0	48	122.0
2	50	5.0	15	38.0	32	81.5	49	124.5
2½	65	6.5	16	40.5	33	84.0	50	127.0
3	75	7.5	17	43.0	34	86.5		
3½	90	9.0	18	46.0	35	89.0		
4	100	10.0	19	48.5	36	91.5		
4½	115	11.5	20	51.0	37	94.0		

Crochet Hooks Conversion Chart

U.S.	1/B	2/C	3/D	4/E	5/F	6/G	8/H	9/I	10/J	10½/K	N
Continental-mm	2.25	2.75	3.25	3.5	3.75	4.25	5	5.5	6	6.5	9.0

Annie's®

Published by Annie's, 306 East Parr Road, Berne, IN 46711. Printed in USA. Copyright © 2018 Annie's. All rights reserved. This publication may not be reproduced in part or in whole without written permission from the publisher.

RETAIL STORES: If you would like to carry this publication or any other Annie's publication, visit AnniesWSL.com.

Every effort has been made to ensure that the instructions in this publication are complete and accurate. We cannot, however, take responsibility for human error, typographical mistakes or variations in individual work. Please visit AnniesCustomerService.com to check for pattern updates.

ISBN: 978-1-59012-970-8

1 2 3 4 5 6 7 8 9